DUNCAN BALL & IAN BALL

The Spy Code Handbook

Illustrations: STEPHEN CASE

Template diagrams: DIANA KUREEN

ANGUS & ROBERTSON PUBLISHERS

Introduction

Welcome to the wonderful world of secret writing. On the following pages you'll find various types of easy-to-make code and cipher machines. Some of them are based on devices that have been used by spies for centuries and others are the products of our own twisted minds. In either case, you'll find that they'll give you hard to crack secret writing—whether it's for passing notes in class, writing postcards that no one but you or your friends can read or just for keeping a diary that only you can decipher.

In addition to the standard codes and ciphers supplied in this book, at the end of each chapter we've demonstrated ways of making your own special machines to write codes that even other owners of this book will have trouble cracking. This way, when you're communicating with a friend, the two of you will be the only ones who can read each other's messages.

How to Use This Book

To make the code and cipher machines in this book, you will need:

• thin cardboard (not corrugated)
• sharp pencil
• pair of compasses
• glue
• cutting knife or single-edge razor
• steel ruler
• small paper fasteners

All the code and cipher machines in this book can easily be made by transferring the designs to cardboard and then cutting them out according to the instructions. Thin cardboard, such as a manila folder or a breakfast cereal package, makes an ideal construction material.

You could cut the designs directly from the book but then you'd also cut the things on the back of the page. Besides, why ruin a good book when you can keep it intact and use it over and over again?

The easiest way to transfer the designs is to photocopy them and then glue the photocopy to the cardboard. (The publisher grants the owner of this book permission to photocopy the designs for his or her private use only.) If you don't have the use of a photocopier, trace the designs and glue the tracing paper to cardboard.

You will need a sharp pencil, a pair of compasses, and a steady hand. You only need inexpensive compasses, available at most newsagencies and stationers. These are important, not only to draw circles, but also to punch small holes when required.

Use whichever glue gives a good even coating without leaving the paper and cardboard permanently warped. In general, the glues that you apply from a stick or a roller give a more even coating than the ones applied by brush.

Once the glue has dried, cut along the designs. The best way to do this is with a small, pencil-size cutting knife (for example, the Stanley S.M. Cutter) or a single-edge razor. Some of the cutting can be done with scissors but a cutting knife or razor is best for the fine work. Cut along a steel ruler for greater accuracy. Don't use a wooden or plastic ruler, as your cutter will gouge and ruin it.

WARNING: Exercise care when cutting with a cutting knife and ruler. Don't let your fingers stray over the edge of the ruler where they might be cut. And don't forget to put newspaper underneath your work to protect desks and tables from sharp blades.

Some of the code machines will require pins through the middle to hold them together. Very small paper fasteners—the smaller the better—are available from some newsagencies or stationers. If you can't find very small paper fasteners, you can use a thumb tack (drawing pin) stuck into a small piece of wood or a cork on the other side. This will work very well but a cork on the back of your code machine will make it too cumbersome to keep in a shirt pocket.

Remember, the more care you take in making your code machines, the better they'll work.

Some Tips about Codes and Ciphers

In general, in this book, we have used the convention of writing the code or cipher in all capitals and the message itself in lower case. The reason for this is simply to avoid confusion.

Message:

help! they're coming to get me!

Cipher:

(this one written with Alberti Wheel, Leon R, explained on page 5):

ZQOK! LZQA'CQ WYJHUV LY VQL JQ!

Most writers would hide the message further by taking out the punctuation and the spaces between words:

ZQOKLZQACQWYJHUVLYVQLJQ

Or they would hide it even better by putting the enciphered message into groups of four or five letters. This has two advantages:
1. No one knows which code or cipher machine you've used. As you begin to use the machines in this book you will see why this is so.
2. It's easier to handle.

ZQOKL ZQACQ WYJHU VLYVQ LJQ

If you are sending messages to a **code partner**, you'll have to make sure that he or she:
1. has the same code or cipher machine that you do,
2. knows which code or cipher you're using and,
3. knows **how you are using the machine**.

It's best to communicate all this separately from the code message itself. But there are tricky ways of putting the "key" to deciphering the message **with the message** without anyone knowing what you've done. For example, we've given all our sample code and cipher machines names like "Ann" or "Arthur". You could rename the same devices "oak" and "pine", or "rabbit" and "sparrow", or simply "1045" and "2567". Even if you include the name with your cipher message, no one but your code partner will know what it means.

Similarly, you could work out a signal with your friend to tell how a certain code or cipher machine is being used. We've called our sample Alberti Wheel "Leon" after Leon Alberti. "Leon L" would indicate that the message was written with the message letter "a" on the cipher letter "L". "Leon 12" could mean the same thing because "L" is the twelfth letter of the alphabet.

In any event, we're sure that once you've made a few of these machines you'll figure out ways of using them that will baffle the best code-breakers. So, happy ciphering!

Alberti Wheel

The Alberti Wheel was named after the fifteenth-century Italian architect and code and cipher expert, Leon Battista Alberti. It is a simple machine that takes the work out of writing **substitution ciphers**—ciphers in which a letter, number or symbol is substituted for each letter of your message.

Making an Alberti Wheel

1.
Copy the inner and outer wheels (figures A and B), and glue them to cardboard.

2.
Cut them out.

3.
To fasten the smaller, inner, wheel onto the larger one, make a hole through the centres with the point of a pair of compasses and then attach them with a small paper fastener (the smaller the better).

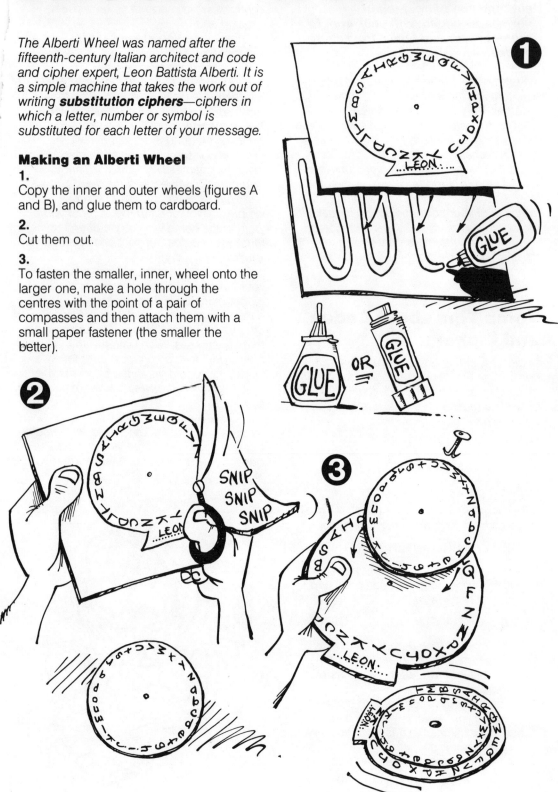

Using an Alberti Wheel

Enciphering with an Alberti Wheel is dead easy. Just put the message letter "a" on the inner wheel opposite any letter on the outer wheel; for example, the letter "Z". Now keep the wheel in that position and simply substitute the letters of your message for the cipher letters on the outside wheel opposite them. Make sure you read the letters right way up otherwise your "M" could become a "W". Here's an example using "Leon Z":

Message:

> *what is round and angry? a vicious circle*

"Leon Z" cipher:

> EYZR KI AMGTX ZTX ZTUAF? Z WKPKMGI PKAPDO

NOTE: "Leon Z" simply means that you are using the Leon wheel with the message letter "a" (on the inner wheel) opposite the cipher letter "Z" (on the outer wheel). "Leon P" would mean that you are using the Leon wheel with the message letter "a" opposite the cipher letter "P". By rotating the wheel, Leon will give you twenty-six different ciphers.

How to Make Your Message Harder to Crack

The good thing about the Alberti Wheel is that it's easy to use. The bad thing is that the cipher is easy to crack. To make things more difficult for the would-be cipher-cracker, you could simply write your message backwards. Even if they had our sample Alberti Wheel, "Leon", on hand, they would get a message like:

> elcricsuoiciva?yrgnadnadnuorsitahw

They probably wouldn't guess that this is simply, "what is round and angry? a vicious circle" spelled backwards.

You could also try rotating the wheel a set amount each time you encipher another letter. You could rotate it clockwise one letter each time, or follow some other pattern like 1,2,3,1,2,3, etc. Just make sure your code partner knows what system you're using.

How to Design Your Own Alberti Wheel

We have also included blank Alberti cipher wheels (figures C and D) which you can use to make your own personal wheel. Make an identical one for your code partner. Remember, you don't have to put letters on the outer wheel. You can use numbers or symbols if you wish.

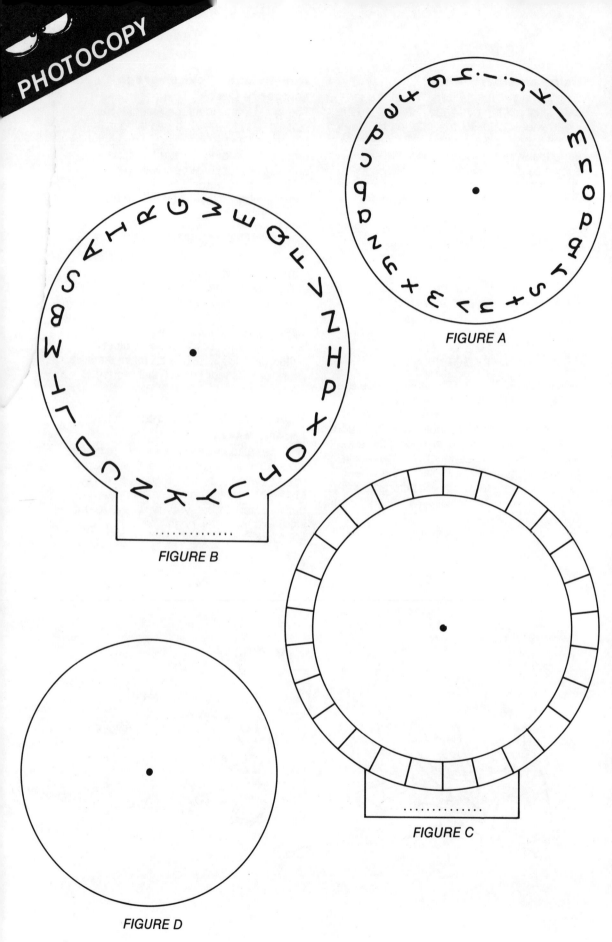

PHOTOCOPY

FIGURE A

FIGURE B

FIGURE C

FIGURE D

Letter Template

Letter Templates are another ancient way of hiding a message on a piece of paper. Unlike an Alberti Wheel, a Letter Template doesn't translate your message into cipher but simply scrambles it in such a way that it can only be read by someone with the same template.

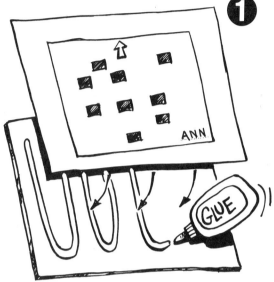

Making a Letter Template

1.
Copy the Letter Template (figure A) which we've called "Ann", and glue the copy to a piece of thin cardboard.

2.
Cut it out with scissors or a cutting knife and a steel ruler.

3.
Remove the boxes inside the template as carefully as possible with a cutting knife or a single-edge razor.

How to Decode a Message

First try reading the message in figure B with the "Ann" template (A). Place it over the letters with the arrow pointing up and copy them down on a piece of paper from left to right, top to bottom. You should get:

betyoucan

Now rotate the template 90 degrees to the right and copy out the letters as before:

tfigureou

Rotate the template another 90 degrees, copy out the letters and then do the same thing again. You should now have:

betyoucantfigureouthowtoreadthisnote

How to Encode a Message

To encode a message, do the same thing in reverse.

1.
Put the template (figure A) on a blank piece of paper with the arrow pointing up. Trace around the template to make a square.

2.
Holding the template in place write the beginning of your message in the blank boxes.

3.
Rotate the template 90 degrees to the right and write in the blank boxes.

4.
Rotate the template 90 degrees to the right each time the boxes are filled.

If your message is long, and you have used the template in all four positions and filled up the square, just draw another square and continue with your message.

If you are left with a partially filled square, put in an "end of message" sign like "ZZ" and then fill the remaining boxes with any letters. Don't ever leave a partially filled square. It will help a code-breaker work out what your template looks like.

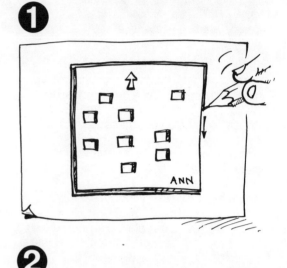

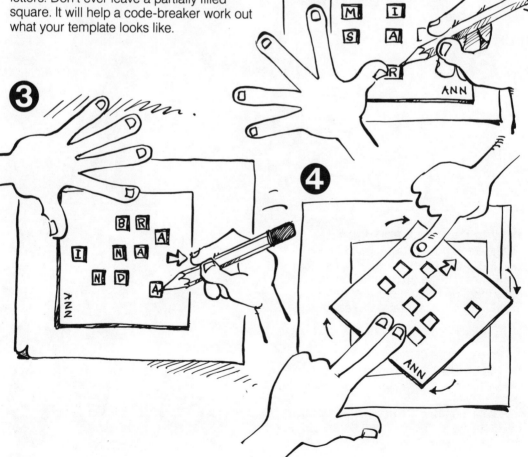

PHOTOCOPY

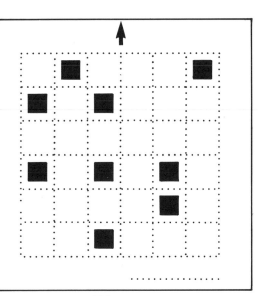

FIGURE A

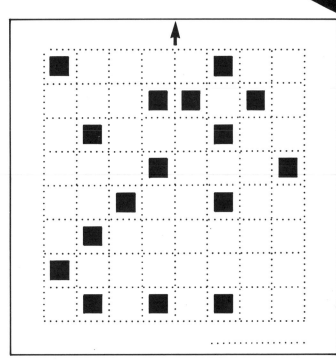

FIGURE C

FIGURE B

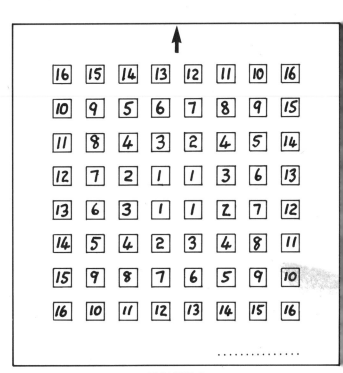

FIGURE D

Making Your Message Harder to Crack

To make your Letter Template message even harder to crack, write the letters in the square out in a line from left to right. The coded message in figure B would become:

DBTTFETHYTHIGOUWRTOIUSCNOEO
OARETNEAU

Your code partner will have to know what you've done, of course, in order to put it back in a square and then read it with the template. The thing to do is to take the same template and trace around all the inner boxes (by rotating the template) till you have a square filled with empty boxes. Then put the letters back in and place the template over the boxes and read it as before.

Instead of left to right, top to bottom, you could copy the coded message out from top to bottom, left to right:

DTGOOEBHOIETTYUUONTTWSOEFH
RCAAEITNRU

Now separate it into five-letter "words":

DTGOO EBHOI ETTYU UONTT WSOEF
HRCAA EITNR U

Another way of making a message trickier to find is **to not rotate the template clockwise**. You could rotate it anticlockwise as you write in the message. Or you could start with the arrow up and then turn it arrow down, then arrow left, then arrow right. And remember, you can always turn the template face down and do the same. In all, there are forty-eight different ways to write a message on a piece of paper using any one template.

We've given you one more Letter Template design in figure C, but why not design your own?

How to Design Your Own Letter Template

Copy figure D and glue it to cardboard as before. You will see that each number occurs four times; that is, there are four "1"s, four "2"s, etc. Cut out one of each number until you have cut out sixteen boxes. It doesn't matter which boxes you cut out as long as **you only cut one of each number**. Try to scatter them around as much as possible so all the boxes aren't in one corner. Now you have your own personal Letter Template. But why stop at one? You could make more and more and more . . .

If you wish to make a smaller template, for example a 6 by 6 template, just cut out one box each of numbers 1 to 9. There's no limit to the size a letter template can be, but they all have to be **square** and they have to have **an even number of rows and columns**. They could be 8 by 8 or 10 by 10 or 12 by 12, and so on. See if you can figure out how to make one that's bigger than the 8 by 8 template in figure D.

KULX TUNY EBS...

Notch Encoder

The Notch Encoder is simple to make and simple to use. Its advantage over other code and cipher machines is that you can write and read a message very quickly.

Making a Notch Encoder

1.
Copy figure A and glue it to a piece of thin cardboard.

2.
Cut it out with scissors, taking care to cut the notches as carefully as possible.

How to Decode a Message

SYSTEM 1: **One notch per line**
Start by reading the message in figure C. Place the Notch Encoder horizontally with the notches pointing downward and its left-hand edge against the vertical line. Now draw it downward, writing down the message letter that corresponds with each notch. You should get the message:

panic

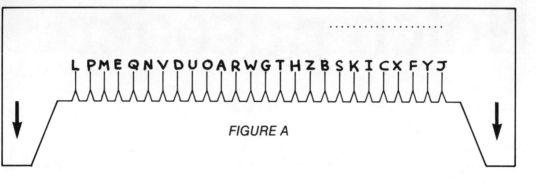

L P M E Q N V D U O A R W G T H Z B S K I C X F Y J

FIGURE A

FIGURE B

SYSTEM 2: **Reading notches from left to right**

Now try reading the message in figure D. This time, on each line we've put as many notches as we could **but only going from left to right**. The first message letter is "s" and we put that mark on the top line. But the second letter, "e", was to the left of "s" so we didn't use it. Instead we moved to the next line and found that we could put down three letters—"e", "n" and "d"—moving from left to right.

Keep reading the notches and see if you can read:

sendmorehelpatonce

Break the message into words and you have:

send more help at once

SYSTEM 3: **Reading notches from left to right and encoding in two directions**

In figure E we've done just the same as we did in figure C except that when we'd moved down five lines, we inverted the page and started back in the opposite direction, using the same lines. System 3 is a good way of putting more information into a small space. The problem with system 3 is that when you are encoding a message you can't be sure when to go back in the opposite direction. The best way is probably to count the number of letters you are encoding and then do a bit more than half of them before starting back.

NOTE: You don't have to follow a vertical line when you're encoding. You can just use the left-hand edge of the paper that you are writing on.

SYSTEM 1 (FIGURE C)

P
A
N
I
C

SYSTEM 2 (FIGURE D)

S
END
MOR
EH
E
LPAT
O
NC
E

SYSTEM 3 (FIGURE E)

S
END
Ǝ MOR
NC EH
O E
LPAT

K SEPB ZYP PUZH FYHUH SUPPOVUP KZ FROPP
K SEPB ZYP PUZH FYHUH SUPPOV UP KZ FROPP
K SEPB ZYP PUZH FYHUH SUPPOVUP KZ FROPP
K SEPB ZYP PUZH FYHUH SUPPOVUP KZ FROPP
K SEPB ZYP PUZH FYHUH SUPPOVUP KZ FROPP
UZH FYUH

How to Encode a Message

Once you have learned to read a message from the examples above, writing a message will be easy.

1.

Start by drawing a straight line down both sides of the paper to use as a guide. (You can use the left-hand edge of the paper as a guide if you wish.)

2.

Now place the encoder against the guideline with its notches pointing down on the top horizontal line. Start by pencilling in a notch opposite the first letter of your message.

3.

If the next letter is to the right of the first one on the encoder, pencil it in without moving the encoder. If it is to the left or is the same letter, move the encoder down a line and continue.

How to Make Your Message Harder to Crack

Notch-encoded messages are relatively easy to crack. Because they are simple substitution ciphers put in the form of notches, an inexperienced code-breaker who knew about notch encoders could probably crack a message, given enough time. So probably the best way to keep it secret is to hide it.

One way to do this is to use small dots instead of notches and to hide them on a printed page. Take a newspaper and move the encoder down the page, leaving small dots on each line right in the middle of the words. The only disadvantage in using dots is that you can encode in one direction only. Also, you'll find it easier to read and to hide the message if you use system 1— only one dot per line. However, with a sheet of newspaper, you can hide quite a long message going in only one direction and using just one letter per line. Unless someone is looking for your secret message, it probably won't be noticed.

Designing Your Own Notch Encoder

There's nothing to it. Simply make another notch encoder using the blank one in figure B and then put your own scrambled alphabet on it. Don't forget to give it a name and to give an identical one to your code partner.

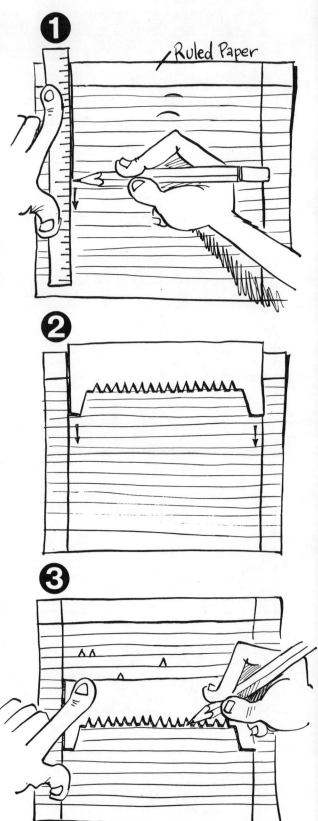

Ruled Paper

Postcode Template

The Postcode Template is a simple device used to hide a message without having to turn it into a cipher. It's a good way to write a postcard to a friend without everyone being able to read it. We've suggested a number of designs but many more shapes and sizes are possible.

Making a Postcode Template

1.
Copy figure A and glue it onto thin cardboard.

2.
Cut around the outer line with scissors.

3.
Cut along the inner line with a cutting knife or single-edge razor until the heart comes loose. Cut out the heart as neatly and evenly as possible.

4.
You will need both the inner and outer pieces.

How to Encode a Message

To read the secret message in figure B, simply place the outside of the "heart" Postcode Template over the written side of the postcard. The first part of the message can now be easily read. Now put the inner piece into the outer piece of the template. Holding the inner piece in place with a finger, remove the outer piece and read the remainder of the message. The message you should get is:

INNER PIECE

This is just a note to say that everything is OK up here in sunny Queensland but that I'll be back in the big smoke before you get this

OUTER PIECE

If there's anything I hate it's someone like that brat of a brother of yours who would read this postcard in a minute if he had the chance

How to Decode a Message

Writing your own message is just a matter of following the example above in reverse but be sure the person you're sending messages to also has the same templates as you and knows which one to use.

1.
Place the outside piece of your Postcode Template over the postcard or paper you wish to write on. Write the first part of your message inside the heart.

2.
Put the inner piece of the template into the outer piece. Holding the inner piece with a finger, remove the outer piece and write the rest of your message.

PHOTOCOPY

FIGURE A

FIGURE B

Suggested shapes

Playfair Mat

The Playfair cipher, named after Baron Lyon Playfair, is a coding system in which pairs of message letters are turned into pairs of cipher letters. It was invented last century and has been used as a military cipher because it is relatively easy to use and difficult to break.

You don't need a machine to write the Playfair cipher. All you need is a pencil and paper. But this device, the Playfair Mat, will allow you to make many different Playfair cipher grids by simply adjusting its ten "control rods".

How to Use a Playfair Grid

The Playfair cipher is easy to use but difficult to describe so read the rules very carefully and follow the examples step by step. Once you learn how to use this cipher you'll never forget it.

First make a Playfair grid. This has five rows and five columns and has the whole alphabet written in the grid boxes. In the sample grid below, we have put the letters in alphabetical order. This is not necessary—**the letters can be in any order as long as the whole alphabet is there**. Notice that there isn't room for both "i" and "j" so these have been placed in the same box. Use either letter. Your code partner will be able to sort out the "i"s from the "j"s in the message. Some people prefer to substitute "j"s for "i"s in their message before they start enciphering.

```
A  B  C  D  E
F  G  H  I/J  K
L  M  N  O  P
Q  R  S  T  U
V  W  X  Y  Z
```

We will use the message "attack now coming" for our example. First take the message and break it up into pairs of letters:

at ta ck no wc om in gz

Because there is an odd number of letters, we have added a "z" at the end to make the final pair.

If you find two of **the same letter**, separate them by putting an "x" between them. The mesage "will you" becomes:

wi lx ly ou

Next take the first pair of letters, "at", and find them in the grid.

CONDITION 1
When the letters are not in the same row or column, use the opposite corners of the rectangle.

Imagine that "a" and "t" are on the corners of a rectangle. The other corners are the cipher letters "DQ". Write the cipher letter "D" first because it's in the same **row** as the first message letter, "a". So "at" becomes "DQ".

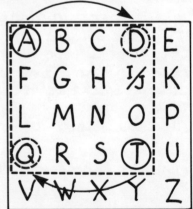

The next two letters of the message are "ta". Again, find them on the grid and find the corners of the imaginary rectangle. As it happens, it's the same square rectangle as before. But this time the cipher letters are "QD" because the "Q" is in the same **row** as the message letter "t". Similarly, the next letters, "ck", become the cipher letters "EH". However the letters "no" **do not** form a rectangle, so they are dealt with according to condition 2.

CONDITION 2

When the letters are in the same row, take the next letter to the right of each letter in that row.

The message letters "no" are in the same row, so we take the **next letters along the same row**—thus "no" becomes "OP".

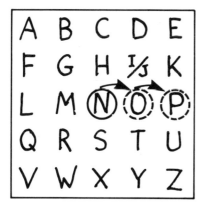

As before, we take the cipher letters in **the same order** as the message letters. If we had the message letters "om", they would become the cipher letters "PN".

NOTE: If you reach the end of the row, simply go around to the beginning again; for example, the message letters "be" would become "CA".

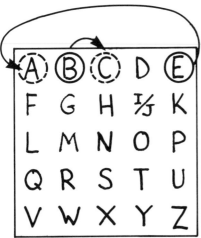

CONDITION 3

When the letters are in the same column, take the letter below each letter in that column.

If your letters are in the same column, the principle is exactly the same as for letters in the same row. The message letters "gr" would become "MW"; "rg" would of course be "WM".

And, if you reach the bottom of a column, go to the top again. The message letter "xh" would become "CN".

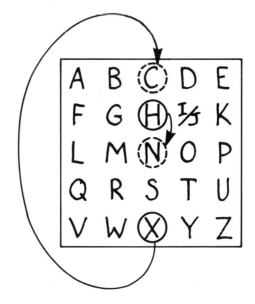

Using the Playfair grid above, our message, "attack now coming", would be:

DQ QD EH OP XB PN HO KW

or, without the spaces that would give away which cipher we are using:

DQQDEHOPXBPNHOKW

Practise putting messages into cipher till you get the hang of it. Decipher the messages the same way.

How to Make a Playfair Mat

The tricky thing about making the mat is cutting the control rods evenly and accurately. If they are cut too thin, they will slide very easily and could fall out. If the rods are too thick, they will be impossible to slide.

1.
Copy the ten control rods (figure A) and the front and back pieces of the mat (figures B and C), and glue them onto thin cardboard.

2.
Cut out the rods and the front and back pieces.

3.
From the front piece (B), cut out the ten small boxes and the large box in the centre. Use a cutting knife and steel rule if possible.

4.
Once all the pieces are cut, weave the rods together into a mat. Use simple under-over weaving. Make sure the rods are in the same order as the ones in the diagram.

5.
Even up the rods and sandwich them between the front and back pieces.

6.
There are twelve short black lines on the front piece of the mat. Staple along these lines as accurately as possible and without stapling the control rods. This completes the Playfair Mat.

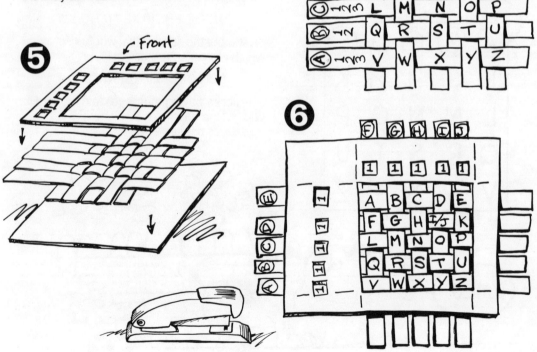

PHOTOCOPY

How to Use a Playfair Mat

As you can see, all you have to do is push and pull the control rods and you will have many completely different Playfair grids. The control rods have either two or three positions and each of the resulting grids will have the whole alphabet. If there is a blank in the grid, you will have pushed or pulled a control rod too far.

NOTE: Be careful not to pull the rods so far that they come out of the mat. If you do, you may have to remove all the staples and take the mat apart to fix it.

Now all you have to do is to tell your code partner which position your control rods are in when you write a message. Your partner will then adjust the control rods of his or her Playfair Mat to the same positions to decipher the message. To specify the position of the control rods, give your partner the numbers in the boxes, listed from rod A to rod J. Our first sample grid (top right) is in position 1 1 1 1 1 1 1 1 1 1. The second grid (bottom right) is in position 1 2 3 1 2 2 3 1 2 1.

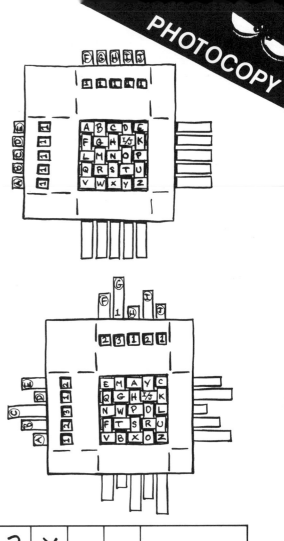

FIGURE A

Rod	Positions			Letters						
J	1	2		K	Ↄ	Ↄ	K			
I	1	2	3	D	Y	O	D	Y	O	D
H	1	2		H	S	S	H			
G	1	2	3	B	W	Σ	B	W	Σ	B
F	1	2		F	ꝺ	ꝺ	F			
E	1	2	3	A	E	C	A	E	C	A
D	1	2		G	I/J	I/J	G			
C	1	2	3	L	P	N	L	P	N	L
B	1	2		R	T	T	R			
A	1	2	3	V	Z	X	V	Z	X	V

PHOTOCOPY

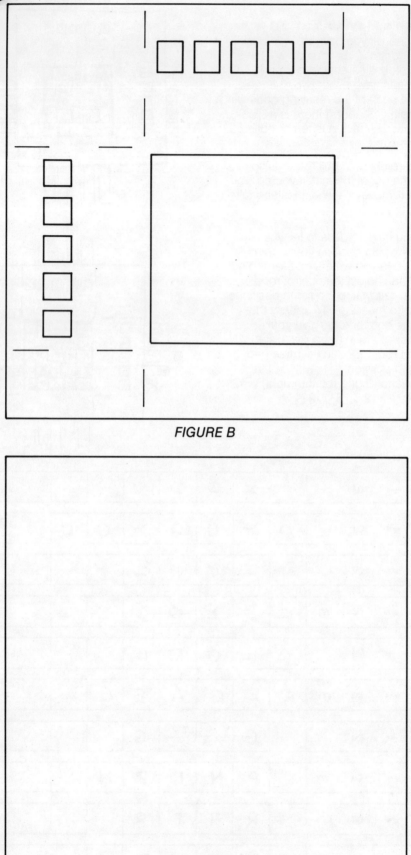

FIGURE B

FIGURE C

Combination Letter Template

The Combination Letter Template is a variation on the simpler, one-piece Letter Template. The principle of hiding the message in plain sight is the same. The message is simply scrambled and can only be read with a similar template. The advantage of the Combination version, which is made in two pieces instead of one, is that any one template can be used in 192 different ways instead of forty-eight ways. By turning one piece of the template while keeping the other piece still, you can create a whole new Letter Template.

Making a Combination Letter Template

1.
Copy the Letter Template pieces (figures A and B) and glue them to thin cardboard.

2.
Cut them out with scissors or a cutting knife and a steel ruler.

3.
Remove the black boxes inside the template pieces as carefully as possible with a cutting knife or a single-edge razor.

4.

Now put both pieces together by punching a hole with a point of your compasses and inserting a paper fastener. You will notice that as you rotate the top piece while keeping the bottom piece stationary, the numbers "1", "2", "3" and "4" will appear in one of the boxes. These indicate the position you start in. Each of these four positions makes a whole new letter template.

5.

Turn the template over and draw an arrow on the back piece (B) like the one on the front piece.

Write the numbers "1", "2", "3" and "4" in the box on the left hand side, three from the top, turning the template 90 degrees for each number.

We've called the front of our sample Combination Letter Template "Jill". Write a code name on the back. What about "Jack" to go with "Jill"?

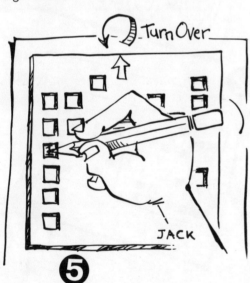

How to Decode a Message

First try reading the message in figure C. Start with the "Jill" facing you, the number 1 showing in the centre box and the arrow pointing up. You might call this "Jill 1 up" when you're communicating with your code partner.

Copy out the first set of letters:

fullmarks

Now turn **the whole template** 90 degrees clockwise, just as you would with the simple Letter Template.

NOTE: Turn both pieces of the template. The number 1 should still be showing.

Continue turning the template and writing down the message. You should get:

fullmarksifyouhavefiguredth
isoutzzea

You can break it up into words.

NOTE: Because we didn't have enough letters to fill the square, we ended the message with "zz" and then filled the remaining boxes with any letters, in this case "ea".

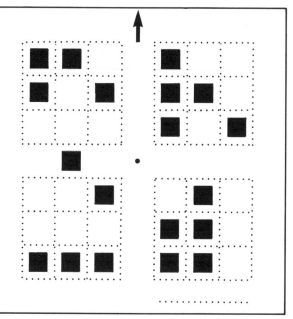

FIGURE A

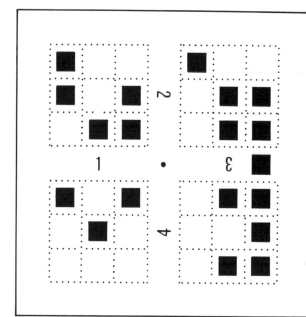

FIGURE B

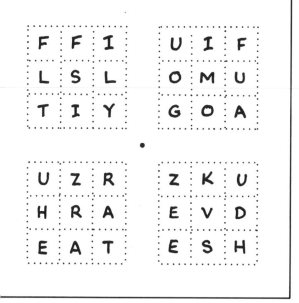

FIGURE C

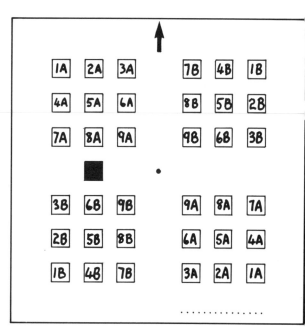

FIGURE D

How to Encode a Message

To encode a message, do the same thing in reverse.

1.
Put the template on a blank piece of paper with the arrow pointing up. Trace around the template to make a square.

2.
Write the beginning of your message in the blank boxes.

3.
Rotate the **whole** template (both pieces) 90 degrees to the right and write in the blank boxes.

4.
Rotate the template another 90 degrees to the right each time the boxes are filled.

If your message is long, and you have used the template in all four directions and filled up the square, just draw another square and continue with your message.

If you are left with a partially filled square, put in an "end of message" sign like "zz" and then fill the remaining boxes with any letters.

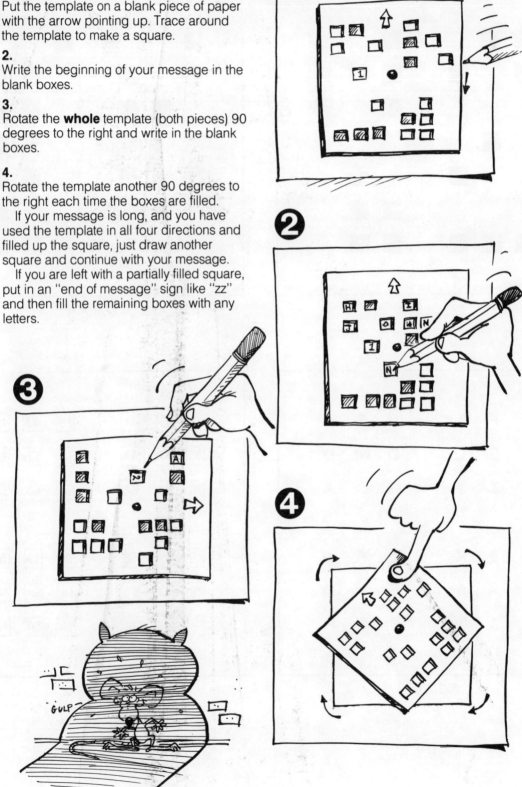

Making Your Message Harder to Crack

As with other Letter Templates, you can make your message harder to crack by changing your letter square into something else. If someone saw figure C, a letter square, they would know what kind of code you were using. If you took the letters from the square and wrote them out on another piece of paper, they wouldn't know what sort of code system you were using. For example, the cipher in figure C would become:

FFIUIFLSLOMUTIYGOAUZRZKUHR
AEVDEATESH

To make the message even harder to decode, you could break it up into five-letter "words":

FFIUI FLSLO MUTIY GOAUZ RZKUH
RAEVD EATES HZZTH

The person you give the message to will have to know what you have done and will have to write it all back in a square just like figure C and then read it with his or her template.

The way to make the square with the blank boxes is simply to put the template down on a piece of paper and trace around each box, rotating the template till the square is filled with empty boxes. Then write the message in the boxes, put the template over the square and start reading.

Instead of going from left to right, top to bottom, as we did above, you could copy the message out from top to bottom, left to right:

FLTUHEFSIZRAILYRATUOGZEE
IMOKVSFUAUDH

And remember, you don't have to always turn the template 90 degrees clockwise. You can turn it anticlockwise or you can turn it from "arrow up" to "arrow down" to "arrow left" to "arrow right". You could start with the arrow down or to the right or left, for that matter. And, of course, you can make four completely different templates by turning the top piece in relation to the bottom piece. Believe us, there are 192 different ways to use a Combination Letter Template.

FIGURE E

How to Design Your Own Combination Letter Template

The key to designing your own template is in figures D and E. Copy these figures and glue them to thin cardboard. You'll notice that each box in figure D, the **upper piece**, is labelled with a number and a letter. Start by cutting out either both the "1A"s **or** both the "1B"s from figure D. Now cut out either both the "2A"s **or** both the "2B"s. Continue to "9A" and "9B". You will have cut out eighteen numbered boxes. Cut out the black box. Don't worry if you make a mistake. You can patch a hole with paper or tape.

Now place the upper piece (D) on the **lower piece**, figure E. Punch a hole through the middle and attach the two pieces with a paper fastener. With the arrow on the upper piece pointing upwards, write an "X" in one of the boxes with a "1" in it. Without moving the top piece, place "X"s on one of the "2"s, one "3", one "4", and so on through to "9".

Now rotate the top piece 90 degrees and again put an "X" on one number "1", one number "2", and so on to number "9" again.

Now stop. Take the two pieces apart and cut out all the boxes with numbers that you've marked with an "X". Also cut the black box on the right.

Put the pieces together once and for all, turn the template over and put an arrow on the back and the numbers "1", "2", "3" and "4" in the hole which was the black box to mark the four positions of the template. You now have your own, personal, Combination Letter Template.

Jefferson Wheel

When the third president of the United States, Thomas Jefferson, invented this very clever way of enciphering messages, the cipher must have seemed unbreakable. It was so good that it was used as a military cipher, even as recently as the First World War.

We now know that the Jefferson Wheel system is not unbreakable but it is very difficult to crack because it is a multiple-substitution cipher. This means that a given letter, for example "a", might be enciphered as "C" and then "X" and then "T" all in the same message, making it very hard to guess which letter might be which.

Jefferson's original machine had a number of cylinders strung together on a rod. To simplify making the wheel we've flattened the cylinders out into discs but the principle is exactly the same.

Making a Jefferson Wheel

1.
Copy the six discs and the guide (figure A) and glue them to thin cardboard.

2.
Cut them out with scissors.

3.
Poke a hole through the centre of each disc and the guide where indicated with a pair of compasses and then put a paper fastener through all seven pieces to join them. Don't try pushing the point of your compasses through all the pieces at once, as you could hit your hand as well.

It is very important to align the holes as accurately as possible. One way to do this is to stack up all the discs, one on top of the other, with the guide on top and then drive a nail through the centre of the stack with a hammer.

The six discs and the guide should all be able to turn freely. Now you have made your own Jefferson Wheel.

PHOTOCOPY

FIGURE A

How to Encode a Message

This is how to encipher the following message using a Jefferson Wheel:

today is what will be yesterday and was tomorrow

First break up the message into blocks of six letters. Fill out the last letters of the block by adding a double letter like "zz" and then any other letters if they are needed to make a block of six. (Adding double letters, like the "zz"s, doesn't make your cipher easier to break unless the code-breaker knows what you're doing and which letters you're using.) This gives you:

todayi swhatw illbey esterd ayandw astomo rrowzz

Now turn the discs of the Jefferson Wheel till one of the rows reads "todayi", reading **from the centre** (figure B). To put these letters into cipher, we could write down **any** of the other rows. We could use the row before it, "FZFBDH", or the row after it, "RQOVPJ".

As long as your code partner knows which one you are using, it doesn't matter which you choose. But let us take the row of cipher letters four rows before. We will call this "Jeff −4". (Four rows *after* the message line would be "Jeff +4".) This gives:

QMVXOE

Then turn the discs till you have the message letters "swhatw" in a row (figure C). The row of cipher letters four rows before this is:

GKRXRS

Now turn the discs till you have the message letters "illbey" in a row. The row of cipher letters four rows before this is:

FXUKDU

Continue putting each block of six letters into a row and copy down the corresponding cipher row. The complete coded message will be:

QMVXOE GKRXRS FXUKDU XZPZPZ UCMWWS UZPLJK HFNBXU

How to Decode a Message

To decode a message, carry out the procedure in reverse. For example, take the letters "FXUKDU" from the coded message above. Turn the discs till you have these cipher letters in row. Now, because you know that your partner has used the "Jeff −4" code, you will count *forward* four rows. This gives "illbey", the third group of letters in our message.

Making Your Message Harder to Crack

Instead of each block of six cipher letters always being four rows back (−4), you could have the first block of letters four rows back (−4) and the second block two rows forward (+2) and the third block one row forward (+1), then repeat this −4, +2, +1, −4, +2, +1, −4, +2, +1, etc.

How to Design Your Own Jefferson Wheel

This is not as tricky as it seems. Using tracing paper, trace all six discs. Also trace the straight lines between the letters—**very carefully**. Now write in your own scrambled alphabets and paste them to cardboard. Don't forget to make an exact copy for your code partner.

NOTE: Don't write your letters in soft pencil. Use ink that won't smudge. Remember that your thumbs will be all over them when you turn the discs.

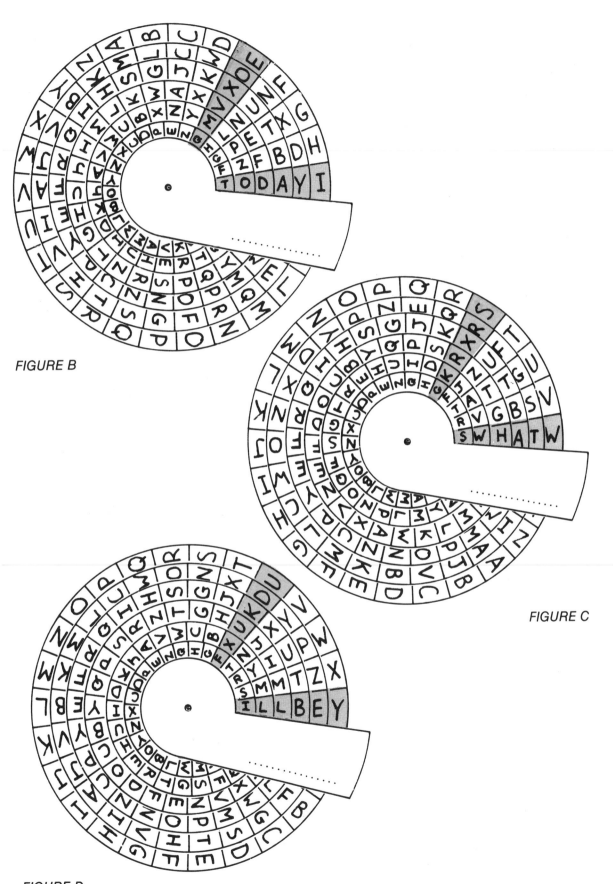

FIGURE B

FIGURE C

FIGURE D

Word Template

A Word Template works the same way as a Letter Template. The message is written out in the boxes of the template and the result is a jumbled mess of words that can only be read by someone with a similar template.

Making a Word Template

1.
Copy the Word Template, figure A, which we've called "Rocky", and glue the copy to a piece of thin cardboard.

2.
Cut it out with scissors or a cutting knife and steel ruler.

3.
Remove the boxes inside the template as carefully as possible with a cutting knife or a single-edge razor.

4.
Turn the template over and write "3" on the bottom edge and "4" on the top edge. (Note that "3" will be on the same edge as "2" and "4" on the same edge as "1" on the front.)

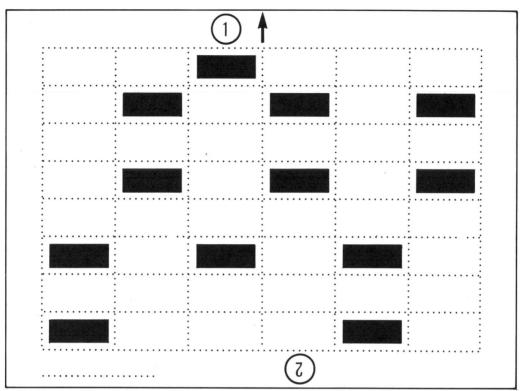

FIGURE A

only	some	use	to	see	one's
break	this	up	word	any	tem
a	nose	mass	unless	of	they
big	plate	words	to	and	hide
have	words	the	that	same	don't
a	fill	mess	in	age	all
tem	make	plate	sense	they	rem
right	the	ember	will	under	blanks

FIGURE B

PHOTOCOPY

Using a Word Template

1.
Place "Rocky" with the arrow up over the words in figure B. You should be able to read:

> use this word tem plate to hide a mess age right under

2.
Now rotate the template 180 degrees (till the arrow is pointing straight down) and continue reading:

> some one's nose unless they have the same tem plate they will

3.
Now turn it over, arrow pointing down. The message should read:

> only see a mass of words that don't make sense rem ember

While the template is in this position, the number "3" will be at the top.

Rotate the template 180 degrees, still with the face down ("4" will be at the top) and continue reading the message:

> to break up any big words and fill in all the blanks

Note that we haven't used capital letters or punctuation, as this makes the code more difficult to crack. If your message is longer than forty-eight boxes (the message square), just start another square. If your message ends before you've filled a whole square, write a word that you and your code partner know will signal the end of the message—for example, "mane"—and then fill the rest of the boxes with any words. Don't leave any blank boxes in a square, as they make your code easier to crack.

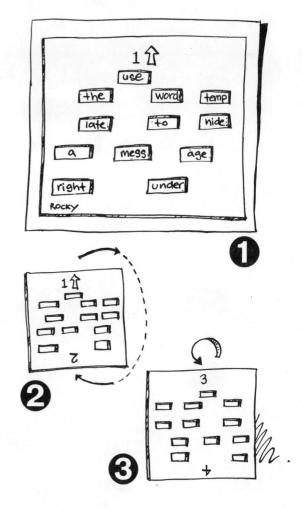

Making Your Message Harder to Crack

One way to make your message harder to crack is by **not breaking up the words**. If you have a word like "remember" that won't fit in a box, write the first part in the box, then lift the template and finish writing the word. You may have to write it in small letters so you don't run into the next word. Of course the person reading it will also have to lift the template to read the whole of "remember". Putting in only whole words prevents a codebreaker from looking for broken words, like "rem" and "ember", and thus working out the positions of two of the template's boxes. If there were a lot of broken words, the codebreaker could work out what your whole template looked like and then read all your secret message.

As with the other templates in this book, once the message is written on the square it can be rewritten on another piece of paper to keep anyone from knowing that

PHOTOCOPY

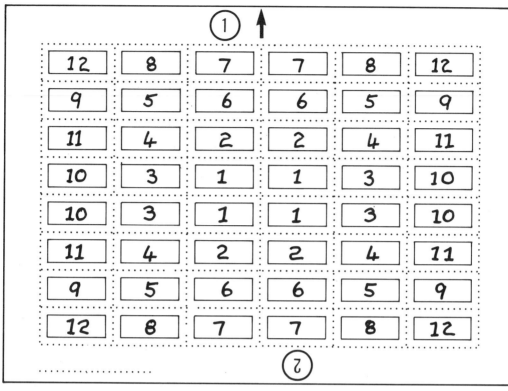

FIGURE C

you were using a Word Template. For example, the message in figure B could be rewritten like this, taking the words from left to right, starting in the top row:

only some use to see one's break this up word any tem a ...

Or it could be rewritten from top to bottom, left to right:

only break a big have a tem right some this nose plate ...

Or you could find a completely different way of rewriting the words. You could start at the second column and go up, for example:

the make fill words plate nose this some ...

And then go on to column 5 and go down it:

see any of and same age they under ...

It's just a matter of working out a pattern with your code partner. Your partner will then have to reconstruct the original square and put the right template over it to read the message.

How to Design Your Own Word Template

Copy figure C and glue it to cardboard as before. Cut out one of each number until you have cut out twelve boxes. It doesn't matter which boxes you cut out as long as you only cut one of each number, but it's best to choose boxes in scattered positions. Now you have your own personal Word Template. Make another exactly the same for a friend, giving both templates the same name, and then make more, and more and more ...

We will leave it to you to figure out how to make bigger, more powerful, templates. Yes, it **is** possible.

Pentagon

Our Pentagon is similar to the Alberti Wheel except that it gives a polyalphabetic substitution cipher instead of a simple, mono-alphabetic substitution cipher. This means that with the Alberti Wheel, any given letter of your message, for example the letter "b", will have the same cipher letter, for example "V", all the way through the message. With the Pentagon (as with the Jefferson Wheel), the letter "b" might be "V" and then "O" and then "P", etc., all in the same message. This makes a Pentagon cipher much harder to crack.

Making a Pentagon

1.
Copy figures A and B and glue them to thin cardboard.

2.
Cut them out with scissors.

3.
Poke a hole through the centre of each figure using your compasses and join them with a paper fastener.

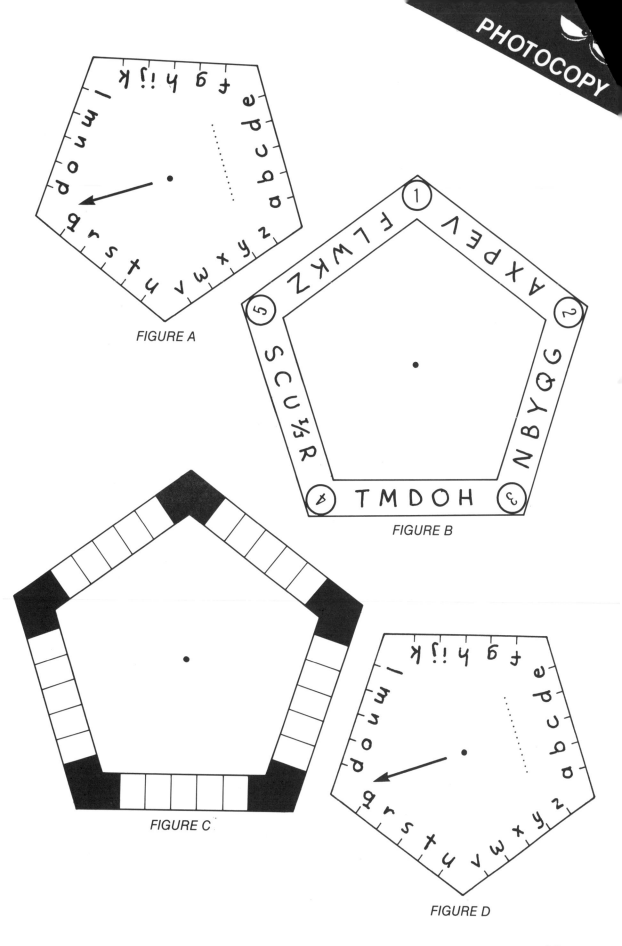

FIGURE A

FIGURE B

FIGURE C

FIGURE D

37

Using a Pentagon

To encipher a message with a Pentagon, start with the arrow of the inner piece pointing to "1". Find the first letter of your message on the inner piece and write down the letter on the outer piece: for example, on our sample Pentagon, which we've called "Ian", "w" becomes "C".

Now turn the inner piece so that the arrow is on "2", and read off your next letter; for example, "h" becomes "D".

Now turn the arrow to "3" and keep going turning the inner piece for each letter till you have finished your message.

NOTE: You'll notice that "i" and "j" are together on both pieces of the Pentagon. We had to do this because being a five-sided figure the Pentagon divides evenly into twenty-five sections only, so two letters of the twenty-six in the alphabet had to double up. Just use either letter in your coded message. It will be obvious to your code partner which is the correct letter to use when he or she is deciphering the message.

Using Pentagon "Ian", the message:

> what does a ghost take for a sore throat—coffin drops

becomes:

> CDFO QERY A XYQYO JTHZ FKL S YJCH EUMKTE—WJANOD ECEGY

NOTE: Because you might forget to turn the inner piece, or you might turn it twice by mistake, and thereby make a mess of the message, try putting the numbers over the letters before you begin putting it into cipher.

> 1 2 3 4 5 1 2 3 4 5 1 2 3 4 5 1 2 3 4 5
> w h a t d o e s a g h o s t t a k e f o

Similarly, when you're about to decipher a message, start by writing in the numbers over the cipher letters. This will keep you from getting muddled up.

> 1 2 3 4 5 1 2 3 4 5 1 2 3 4 5 1 2 3 4 5
> C D F O Q E R Y A X Y Q Y O J T H Z F K

And if you're deciphering a message and suddenly it turns to gibberish, try turning the inner piece back a number or forward a number. The code-writer may have made a simple mistake.

How to Make Your Message Harder to Crack

If someone found your message and they had a copy of our sample Pentagon, "Ian", they'd have no trouble deciphering it. To make it a bit harder to crack, don't turn the inner piece clockwise from 1 to 2 to 3, etc. Work out another pattern and tell it to your code partner. You could turn it anticlockwise, for example, or turn it according to a particular pattern such as "3, 1, 4, 2, 5 3, 1, 4, 2, 5 3, 1, 4, 2, 5," etc. Or even "3, 2, 2, 5 3, 2, 2, 5," etc. (Don't forget to write the numbers over your message letters before you begin.)

Following a pattern like this is, of course, much slower than just rotating clockwise or anticlockwise.

How to Design Your Own Pentagon

We have included two blank Pentagon pieces, figures C and D, so you can design your own Pentagon. Put the alphabet on the inner piece, remembering to put "i" and "j" together, along with an arrow pointing to one corner. On the outer piece write your own scrambled alphabet and number the corners "1" to "5".

"WHAT DOES A GHOST TWIS XEP K GMQHVL? MUSSY BXOP ... I THINK YOU LOST COUNT"

Triangle Encoder

The Triangle Encoder is very different from the other machines in this book. Instead of encoding a message using letters or numbers, this device leaves a series of lines on a page. These "meaningless" marks only take on meaning when someone has another Triangle Encoder of the same design, like our sample, "Juliet".

This is an easy machine to understand but it's tricky to make, and even trickier if you wish to make two exactly the same.

Making a Triangle Encoder

1.
Copy figure A and glue it to a piece of thin cardboard.

2.
Cut out the triangle using scissors.

3.
Cut out the five black "slots" as accurately as possible. You'll need a single-edge razor—or, better still, a cutting knife—and a steel ruler to do this. Put a hole through the centre using your compasses.

If you are going to make two Triangle Encoders, one for you and one for a friend, try cutting them both together—one on top of the other—to make sure they're exactly the same.

How to Decode a Message

First try reading the letters in figure B. Place the "Juliet" Triangle Encoder on the triangle with the arrow pointing up at the dot and you will see three horizontal bars through the slots. Look at figure D and you will find the same pattern opposite the letter "t". Now turn the Triangle clockwise to the next position. You will find the pattern of bars which matches the letter "h". Turn it again and you'll find "e". So, figure B says "the". (Note: Ignore those sections of bars which cross the slots diagonally.)

Try the same with figure C starting from the left triangle. Then move to the next triangle but, this time, point the arrow on "Juliet" down, towards the dot in the figure.

Then continue to the third triangle. You should get the message: "meetatone", which is "meet at one".

When decoding a message, we find that it's easier to just write down each pattern and decode the marks afterwards.

How to Encode a Message

1.
Trace a line around your Encoder to form a triangle.

2.
With the arrow pointing upwards, fill in the bars which represent the first letter of your message, using the key given in figure D. The best way to fill in the bars is with a thick pen or crayon.

3.
Turn your Encoder clockwise and fill in the bars which represent the second letter of your message.

4.
Turn the Encoder clockwise again and fill in the bars which represent your third message letter.

5.
Draw another triangle, pointing down this time, and continue, starting with your Encoder in the down position.

You could draw all the triangles you will need for your message before you start encoding. As there are three letters per triangle, count the number of letters in your message, divide by three and the result is the number of triangles you will need. If you are writing a message that will fill a lot of triangles, you can string the triangles together with the first one pointing up and the second one pointing down and so on, just as we have done in figure C.

You can also encode a message without drawing triangles. Each time you begin a new set of three letters, you can spin the Encoder around its centre, putting a dot through the centre hole for your code partner to use when decoding the message.

When you fill in the slots, some of the ink or crayon will go on the paper around each slot. If you have cut your Encoder accurately, you will be able to turn it dirty-side down and read the message from the clean side.

How to Make Your Message Harder to Crack

To make the message harder to crack, don't rotate the Triangle clockwise. Try rotating it anticlockwise, or alternate from one to the other with each new triangle.

Another thing you can do is to change the code. Make your own by putting your own scrambled alphabet in the boxes in figure D opposite the patterns.

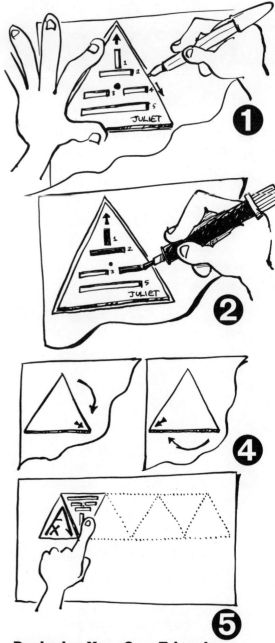

Designing Your Own Triangle Encoder

This is very tricky. Don't attempt it unless you're feeling very brave. If you are, you can design your own encoder in any shape, using the same principle we have used for the Triangle Encoder. Just make sure you have five slots and that when you rotate your encoder, none of the lines made in one position show up when you turn it to another position. If you make it symmetrical, you'll be able to turn it over to the "clean" side as with "Juliet". (But this is so tricky that we don't recommend it.) Now work out a code as in figure D.

PHOTOCOPY

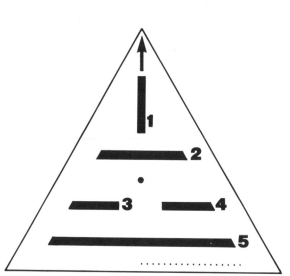

FIGURE A

FIGURE B

FIGURE C

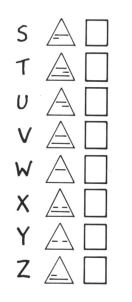

A ☐ J ☐ S ☐
B ☐ K ☐ T ☐
C ☐ L ☐ U ☐
D ☐ M ☐ V ☐
E ☐ N ☐ W ☐
F ☐ O ☐ X ☐
G ☐ P ☐ Y ☐
H ☐ Q ☐ Z ☐
I ☐ R ☐

FIGURE D

Cipher-Stream Wheel

The Cipher-Stream Wheel is an easy machine to make but it takes some thought to use it to its full advantage. As with the Alberti Wheel, it begins as a simple-substitution cipher but then is turned into a stream cipher, making it much harder to crack. But small mistakes in writing stream ciphers (just as with the stream cipher written with the Relativity Slide) cause problems when it comes to deciphering.

Making a Cipher-Stream Wheel

1.
Copy the figures A and B and glue them to thin cardboard.

2.
Cut out the discs with scissors.

3.
Using a single-edge razor or cutting knife and a steel ruler cut out the "cipher", "message" and "column" slots.

4.
Punch a hole through the centres of the two discs and insert a paper fastener to secure them.

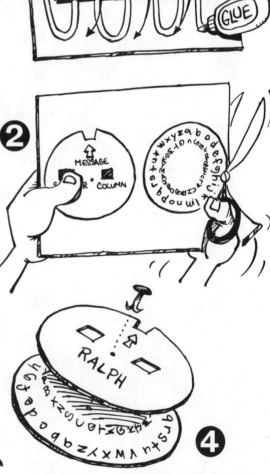

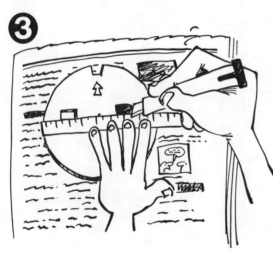

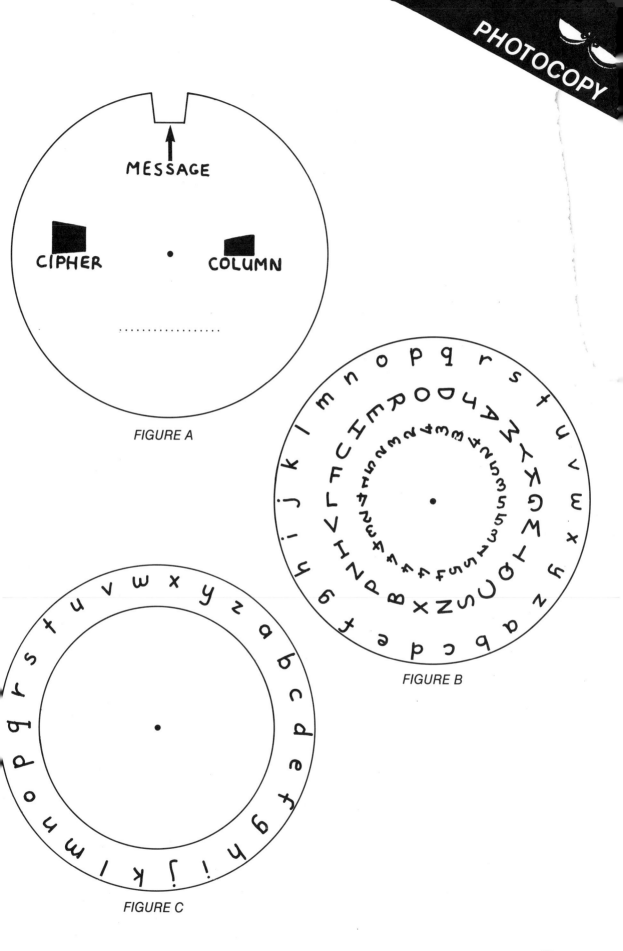

PHOTOCOPY

MESSAGE

CIPHER

COLUMN

FIGURE A

FIGURE B

FIGURE C

Using a Cipher-Stream Wheel

METHOD 1

Write the numbers "1", "2", "3", "4" and "5" across a page. These will be your column numbers. Here is a sample message to work with:

> if you play cards in the jungle beware of cheetahs

Turn the bottom disc till the first letter of the message, "i", appears. Its cipher letter will be "N". Write "N" in column 1. **Always write the first letter of a message in the first column**. Note that the column box on the disc will now say "2". Therefore your next cipher letter will go in column 2. The column box always tells where the **next letter** will go. An easy way to keep track is to put a dot in that column to remind you where the next letter is to go.

Continue through to the end of the message:

1	2	3	4	5
N	Q	P	V	A
S	Y	Y	A	R
X	I	N	G	L
K	E	T	U	W
D	C	T	H	I
V	P	T	R	T
T	S	T	Y	Q
E		H	U	G
Y			S	

Using this method, the column lengths will not be even. Our sample wheel, "Ralph", is specially designed to make them as even as possible but they'll always be somewhat ragged, as above.

To decipher the message just do the same thing. Turn the bottom disc until the first cipher letter, "N", appears. This gives the message letter "i" and tells you which column to go to for your next cipher letter—in this case, column 2. The next cipher letter is "Q", which gives message letter "f" and column 5 for your next cipher letter and so on.

NOTE: We have made our "Ralph" wheel in such a way that you can decipher the message by finding the cipher letter in the **message** box at the top and reading the message letter in the **cipher** box to the left. This makes it easier to find the letters because the message letters are in alphabetical order. The column numbers are still correct when you do this.

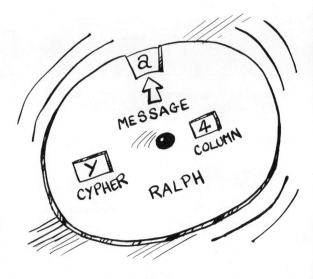

METHOD 2

This is a trickier but much better way to use a Cipher-Stream Wheel. The difference between this and method 1 is that the enciphering starts again after every six letters, so the message can't go too far wrong if there's a mistake. Also, the column lengths come out even, but more on that later.

Number your columns "0", "1", "2", "3", "4" and "5". This time, start by putting the first cipher letter in column 0. The **next** cipher letter will go in the column indicated in the column box, so put a line or a dot in that column so you won't forget. Continue filling the columns in a row until you come to a column that already has a cipher letter in it. When this happens you put the cipher in the first empty column. With this method, you fill up a whole row before you go on to the next row. Encoding the following message will make this clear:

> if you play cards in the jungle beware of cheetahs

Find the first message letter, "i", on the wheel. Its cipher letter is "N" which goes in column 0. According to the column box, the **next letter** will go in column 2. Now find the next message letter, "f". The code letter is "Q". Put a "Q" in column 2 and note that the **next letter** will go in column 5.

Keep going till you get to the message letter "u" from "you". Its cipher letter is "R" and it **should** go in column 5. But column 5 already has the cipher letter "A" in the first row. So the "R" goes in the first empty column which, in this case, is column 1.

The next message letter, the "p" from "play", becomes the cipher letter "L" and also should go in column 5. So this time the next "free" column is column 3. When a row is full, go on to the next row down and **put the first cipher letter in column 0** just as if you were starting a new message.

Using this method, our message becomes:

0	1	2	3	4	5
N	R	Q	L	V	A
P	G	Y	Y	A	U
W	E	I	N	H	S
T	X	C	P	R	I
T	K	D	T	Y	U
T	V	G	S	T	Q
T	E	Y	H	S	Z

Making Your Message Harder to Crack

If you leave your enciphered letters in columns it will be a tip-off to anyone who has this book that you're using a Cipher-Stream Wheel. So why not rewrite them? Take the columns from the cipher described in method 1, for example, and string them out reading down the columns, remembering to put in something— perhaps a "/"—to tell your code partner where a column ends.

The enciphered message would then look like this:

NSXKDVTEY/QYIECPS/PYNTTTTH/
VAGUHRYUS/ARLWITQG

Similarly, you could take the encoded message described in method 2 and rewrite it by listing the enciphered letters across the rows:

NRQLVAPGYYAUWEINHSTXCPRIT
KDTYUTVGSTQTEYHSZ

NOTE: In the example used here, the encoded message filled out all six columns evenly. If, however, there were letters missing at the bottoms of any rows, a symbol (for example "/") could be used to fill them out.

Now, just to make it even more difficult, break up the message into **five** letter groups:

NRQLV APGYY AUWEI NHSTX CPRIT
KDTYU TVGST QTEYH SZ

How to Design Your Own Cipher-Stream Wheel

We've included a disc (figure C) with only the message alphabet around it, for you to make your own Cipher-Stream Wheel. All you have to do is take a top disc, like our sample (A), and attach it using a paper fastener. Simply write a scrambled alphabet of cipher letters in the box on the left as you turn the bottom disc from letter to letter. Don't forget to put in a number from "1" to "5" in the column box as you go. Any number will do.

NOTE: If you wish to be able to decipher a message using the message box for the cipher and the cipher box for the message, as we did when we made the "Ralph" disc, then make sure when you put the cipher letter "A" equal to the message letter "t" that you also make the cipher letter "T" equal to the message letter "a", and so on. That way you can go back and forth. If you do use this system, you must put the same column for A=t as for T=a.

Relativity Slide

A Relativity Slide is easy to understand and easy to make. One difficulty is that you'll be writing a **stream cipher**, and when you write a stream cipher, one tiny error can make the rest of your message meaningless. Also, your enciphered message will be in upper and lower case letters. If your code partner confuses your small "c" with your capital "C", for example, the message could be lost. In other words, extreme care is needed in writing and deciphering messages when you're using a Relativity Slide. If you have trouble writing upper and lower case letters that look different, you could put a line under, or a dot over, all the capital letters.

Making a Relativity Slide

1.
Copy the slide and its slider (figures A and B) and then glue them to thin cardboard.

2.
Cut the slots in the slider with a knife.

3.
Cut the slide and the slider with scissors or a cutting knife and a steel ruler.

4.
Place the slider on the slide so that the letters appear in the slot and you're ready to go.

5.
Copy the two **code rulers** (figures C and D) which we've called "Arthur" and "Martha", and paste them onto cardboard and cut them out.

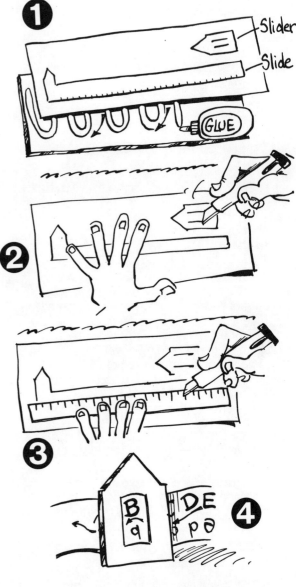

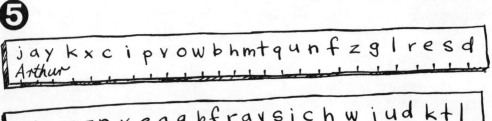

❺

j a y k x c i p v o w b h m t q u n f z g l r e s d
Arthur

p y o m z n x e g q b f r a v s i c h w j u d k t l
Martha

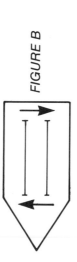

FIGURE A

FIGURE B

FIGURE C

ARTHUR...... j a y k x c i p v o w b h m t g u n f z g l r e s d

FIGURE D

MARTHA...... p y o m z h x e g g b f r a v s i c h w j u d k t l

FIGURE E

47

Using a Relativity Slide

This might sound complicated but it's not. Follow the instructions step by step and do the examples and you'll catch on straight-away.

First write your message out on a piece of paper. Then select a **code ruler**; for example, the one we've called "Arthur". Write the first letter of your message again. **The first letter of your message is also the first letter of your cipher.**

For the second letter, place the "start" pointer on the first letter on the "Arthur" ruler and then move the slider along the slide till it reaches the second letter of your message. The cipher letter is either the upper case letter in the box on the slider or the lower case one depending on whether you have to move from left to right or right to left. If your next message letter is to the right of the last message letter, hold the slide below the rule and move the slider to the right to the new letter. Your cipher letter will be the upper case letter in the box in the slider. If your next message letter is to the left of the last message letter, hold the

slide above the rule and move the slider to the left to the new letter. Your cipher letter will be the lower case letter in the box in the slider. Follow the examples below and you'll see what we mean.

NOTE: If you have a double letter in your message, use the cipher letter "A" or "a" for the second letter.

EXAMPLE 1

1.
Your message starts with "yes". The first letter of your cipher will be capital "Y". Now place the "start" pointer on the "y" on "Arthur" and move the slider out to "e". Read the next cipher letter from the box on the slider. Since you moved from left to right when you went from "y" to "e", the letter is the upper case letter, the "V".

2.
Now do the same going from "e" to "s" and your cipher letter is "B". Thus "yes" becomes "YVB".

EXAMPLE 2
Use the "Arthur" code ruler to encode the message "yet".

The first steps are exactly the same as for example 1 but to go from "e" to "t", **you have to turn the slide upside down above the code ruler** and measure from

right to left. (You'll notice that the **only** way you can put the "start" pointer on "e" and the slider on "t" is to turn the Relativity Slide upside down—see figure on top of next page.) The third letter then is the lower case letter in the slider box, "j"; so "yet" becomes "YVj".